Early Stores and Markets

Bobbie Kalman

The Early Settler Life Series

Toronto
New York

Crabtree Publishing Company

To Samantha, my daughter, who fills my days with love

Special thanks to *Lori Pattenden, Nancy Cook, Trish Holman, Bill Langston, Barbara Snyder, Bill Patterson, Judie Ellis, Andrea Crabtree, Samantha Crabtree, Debbie Scott, Alice Davidson, Mary Elmhirst, Derek Western and Peter Logan.*

Cataloging in Publication Data

Kalman, Bobbie, 1947 –
  Early Stores and Markets

(Early settler life series)
Includes index.
ISBN 0-86505-002-3 hardcover
ISBN 0-86505-004-X paperback

1. Stores, Retail – History. 2. Retail trade – History
I. Title   II. Series

HF5429.K34   381'.1'097   C81-094118-X

350 Fifth Ave, Suite 3308
New York, NY 10118

120 Carlton Street, Suite 309
Toronto, Ontario M5A 4K2

73 Lime Walk
Headington, Oxford 0X3 7AD
United Kingdom

Contents

The man in charge of the supply room of this early settlement was like a storekeeper. He had to keep track of his inventory (the goods he had in stock) in his supply room.

Before there were stores

People started coming to the New World about four hundred years ago. Some people, such as Christopher Columbus and other explorers, came to discover new places for trade. Some came for treasures to take back home with them. Some expected to find new products to trade, such as tea and silk. Others came to make new homes for themselves. Whatever the reason people chose to come here, all of them found hardships and endless work facing them when they finally arrived.

Trees everywhere

The first groups of settlers had to bring with them everything they needed. There was nothing but forests here. There were no houses into which people could move. There were no stores in which to buy supplies. People had to work the moment they set foot on land. Trees had to be cut down. Stumps had to be pulled up. Houses had to be built for shelter and crops had to be planted for food. All the early settlers faced the same hardships and had to help each other to survive.

Working together for a new life

Many of the settlers who came to North America in the seventeenth and eighteenth centuries belonged to religious groups. These groups were not allowed to practice their religions in Europe. Many Puritans, Mennonites and Amish came here to worship God in their own way and to live their lives as they chose. Some groups, such as the Jesuits in New France, came to convert the native people to Christianity.

The whole group usually worked and lived together in a close community, such as a fort or walled area, in order to feel safe and to help each other. Everyone had certain jobs to do for the good of the whole community. Some planted crops, while others made dishes or shoes for the whole community. If someone needed something, it had to be made because there were no stores.

More people, more business

As more ships came from Europe, more goods were brought to the New World. More people also came and towns grew up on the east coast. Some people even grew rich by offering their services to others who could pay. The miller is one example. He ground the grain into flour for everyone in the community. Some men trapped animals for furs and sent the furs back to Europe for gold or for more supplies.

One of the earliest settlements in the New World was Jamestown. This Jamestown resident has been put in the stocks for trying to steal an extra blanket from the suppiy room.

This early settler has the job of making shoes for everyone at this Jesuit settlement called "Ste. Marie Among the Hurons".

In this early walled settlement, the settlers built a waterway inside, so they could paddle right into the settlement if attacked by enemies.

The 18th century millinery shop sold hats and fine fabrics to women. A dressmaker made hats and dresses "to order" there. The term "milliner" came from "Milaner". The best fabrics came from Milan, Italy, and all "Milaners" were thought to be fabric sellers.

17th and 18th century town stores

The early town stores of two hundred years ago sold some beautiful items. Many of the goods were brought from Europe. Some were made right in the town by the many craftsmen. Everything in those days was done by hand or horsepower. There were no machines that could be operated by electricity. If you were to walk into a book-binder's shop or a bootmaker's shop, you would see books and shoes made by hand. It would take a long time to finish one item. People usually ordered what they wanted and then the craftsmen would make it to order. There were few goods that were ready-made.

Many things were stored in barrels in the early days, so the cooper was always busy. There was no cardboard or plastic then.

The shoemaker also made other articles of leather, such as tankards for ale. All the craftsmen worked beside doors and windows for light. There was no electricity.

The bookbinder binds books by hand. On the line above him are the endpapers of the book. They have been dyed in colorful inks and are hanging to dry.

Wigs were worn by men about two hundred years ago. People sold their hair to the wigmaker, who then attached the hairs to a base. The new wig was tied with a bow.

The back room of the apothecary shop was a living room, bedroom, kitchen and storage area as well. The apothecary snoozes as two of his children play a game. His eldest son, who will later take over his shop, works hard on his studies. Herbs, which will later be used as medicine, hang to dry. A skeleton stick stands in the corner of the room.

The apothecary

The apothecary was the town pharmacist or druggist. He was often the doctor as well. He sometimes had a small doctor's office behind his shop. The apothecary shop contained hundreds of beautiful-smelling herbs which were used for different types of illnesses. People in those days did not know much about medicine. Many of the cures were made by guesswork. There were some popular remedies, such as bleeding, amputation and the application of poultices.

Let the bad blood out

People were "bled" to rid their bodies of poisons which made them ill. Most doctors had small instruments with which they were able to make small holes in people in order to allow the "bad blood" to flow out. When a person had an infection that could not be healed on an arm or a leg, doctors cut the arm or leg off. Amputation was more popular with the doctor than with the patient. Poultices were mixtures of herbs ground into a powder and mixed into a paste. The paste was then applied to the infected area. No matter what the remedy was, it was usually painful. There were no anaesthetics in those days.

Sometimes the apothecary even used spells and objects of witchcraft to cure a patient or to make him ill. The "skeleton stick" in the picture was believed to give the apothecary the power to cure or harm any man, woman or child that he treated.

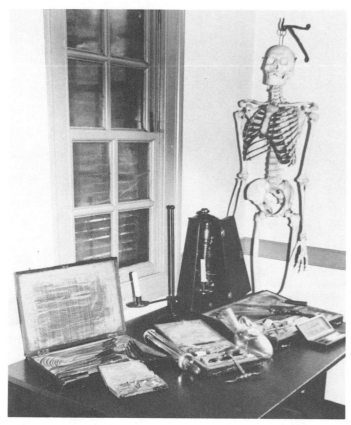

The apothecary was often the doctor as well. In his office we find a skeleton, and tools which look like a carpenter's tools; drills, clamps and saws of all sizes.

The apothecary's tools were the tiny weigh scales and the mortar and pestle with which he ground herbs into powders.

The apothecary's daughter uses the mortar and pestle to make a fine powder for a poultice.

9

These Indians have traded their furs and are now going to take away their supplies in the birchbark canoe. The man on the right is holding a "tump line", which he will put across his forehead, as his friend has done. Then he will carry the heavy pack on his back to the water's edge. The canoe will also be moved to the water and loaded for the long voyage.

These fur hunters had a hard life. They had to walk many miles to the nearest trading post. They had to sleep in the woods at night. They had little food to eat. Some of them grew rich from the silver and supplies they received for their furs. Many, however, got sick on their hard journeys and did not make it back home.

The trading post

Before the coming of new settlers to an area, the only people in the wilderness besides the native people were traders for the Hudson's Bay Company and lumbermen. The trader's job was to go out into the bush and trade with the Indians in return for furs. The beaver pelt was particularly sought after. Once the bristly fur was removed, the soft under-fur was used to make good-looking hats that were in great demand in Europe.

The wilderness connection

The Hudson's Bay Company traded with the Indians for furs right across North America. Other companies did the same. The companies set up trading posts near the native people's trapping areas. At the trading post the fur traders gave the natives beads, blankets, metal knives and pots in exchange for their furs. The native people also traded their furs for food such as salt, sugar, flour and coffee, as well as guns and whiskey. The trading post was usually a small shack in the bush manned by one storekeeper.

Goods traded for goods

The barter system was most often used in the fur trade. The trapper who brought the furs in traded them for other goods that he needed. Very little money was used in those days. When money was used, it was often difficult to know just how much it was worth. People felt much more comfortable trading goods for other goods that they knew they needed.

The opening of the general store was one of the most important events for a newly settled area. The store brought people together to one meeting place to do their trading, to make their business deals and to meet others in the community. People came from all over to trade farm goods for new tools and supplies. A store made an area into a community.

Before a store opened up in an area, people had to make everything they needed for them-selves. The men hunted and looked after the crops and the women cooked the food and made the clothes for the family. Even the children had many chores. The general store made life much easier for everyone. Women could buy some clothes, men supplies and tools.

The General Store opens its doors

The majority of the new settlers came to the New World because they wanted to make new homes here. They were promised land when they came. This land was usually far from any town or civilized area. Settlers had to farm their plots of land and stay alive by growing food as soon as they arrived. They had to make do without the benefits offered by a store. They just owned what they managed to bring with them. Thus, all their possessions were either patched, mended or repaired. If they needed something new, it was homemade. For example, a new dress would be made out of rough material woven by the settler himself or herself. It would not be made of the soft pretty cotton or silk that you could buy in the larger towns.

The first settlers made everything

Everything that was made was made for the family. The crops that were planted were used to feed the family. Sometimes farmers traded extra crops with each other. One farmer may have planted tomatoes and onions, while another planted turnips and potatoes. The two farmers could then share their crops with each other. People also shared tools, animals, wool, fur, leather, milk, butter and bread.

The community connection

However, farmers rarely lived close to each other. They had to travel many miles to do their trading. Everyone was happy when one of the settlers decided to set up a General Store. Now all the farmers in the community could come to one place to trade their goods. They could not only buy the products of the other farmers, but they could also get goods from other places. The General Store opened a whole new life for the settler. It helped to turn separate farms into one community. It brought people together to help each other. And it allowed people to have a contact with the world they had left behind.

The general store was always filled with people. On the left side, the miller and the cabinet maker are making a deal with two farmers. In the center, a villager brags about the deer he shot. The storekeeper is showing some farm children a new book from the city.

The community business center

Villages grew around general stores. Farmers needed many things to be done for them. The settlers who were not farmers set up shops, such as the blacksmith shop, to provide the services needed. Craftsmen, such as the furniture maker, made articles for the settlers and sold some of them at the general store. Skilled people, such as tailors and hairdressers, often provided their services at the store. If a settler needed to borrow horses from the other settlers, the merchant could arrange rentals at the store. Settlers arranged contracts and obtained marriage licences at the store. The village store was the hub or center of activity in an early village.

The village dressmaker offered her dress-making services at the store a couple of times a week.

Women loved to visit the store. There they could find beautiful fabrics, such as silk and soft cotton. The goods at the store reminded them of the big civilized world they left behind.

A contact with civilization

The clothes, tools and most of the food the early settlers used were made by people in the community. The quality of these items was not as fine as of the goods which came from overseas. Women loved to have clothes made from soft cottons and wools, dishes made from real china, and sugar that was refined. These products had to be brought from other places, such as Europe, Asia and the West Indies.

Men could get more efficient tools from the cities. Children loved to look at toys that were made of materials not available in their village. Products at the general store reminded the settlers of the big, civilized world they had left behind. It was wonderful to have some of the memories of civilization brought into the often lonely existence of the early settler.

These children marvel at the new, wonderful toys they see at the general store. The store opened up a whole new world for them.

15

The storekeeper's daughter prepares a letter which will be sent by the next coach. She stamps the letter with the name and place of the store. The receiver will then have to pay for the letter when he or she gets it.

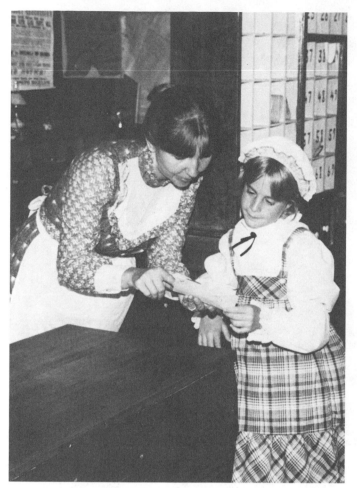

Andrea receives a letter from her cousin John. The storekeeper's wife shows her what rate she has to pay for the letter.

The mail coach was also a passenger coach. Here, one of the villagers greets his niece from a nearby town as shoppers look on.

Pick up your letters at the store!

In the early days there were no telephones. When people left their families behind in Europe, the only contact they had with them was by mail. Friends who lived in different communities in the New World also had to communicate by mail. It took many hours to travel short distances because the roads were rough, if there were any! There were no cars, subways or buses. Travel was dangerous at the best of times. People did not visit each other often. They looked forward to receiving mail.

The mail coach has arrived!

Mail was sent from and received at the general store. The Post Office was usually at the back of the store. Each family had a separate cubby hole into which the storekeeper put incoming mail.
Mail was delivered by coach about every two weeks. As the mail coach arrived, the coachman sounded a large horn blast. The storekeeper sorted the mail and sent the outgoing mail off with the coach.

Write small or pay big!

Today we put stamps on our letters and parcels. There are many different rates. The rates are set by how far the letter or parcel is going and how much it weighs. In the early days, people were charged by the number of pages they received. The rate was paid to the storekeeper when the letter arrived. Often settlers used long sheets of paper and wrote very small so that their relatives or friends would not have to pay very much. There were no envelopes. The pages were folded and sealed with hot wax. The seal of the store showed the town from which the letter came.

The general store was a popular meeting spot for everyone. People sat around the pot-belly stove and discussed community happenings. The store was the village social center.

"I'll see you at the store!"

The general store was the meeting place in the community. There were always people sitting inside or on the bench outside the store. In the winter people sat huddled by the warmth of the pot-belly stove. The villagers sat around, talked, argued or played cards or checkers. On Saturday night the store was usually filled with shoppers. The merchant's whole family helped out in the store. The husband and wife storekeepers shared many duties, such as bookkeeping, stocktaking and selling. The children measured and weighed goods and helped to keep the store clean. Some of the storekeepers even opened small restaurants in the back room of the store.

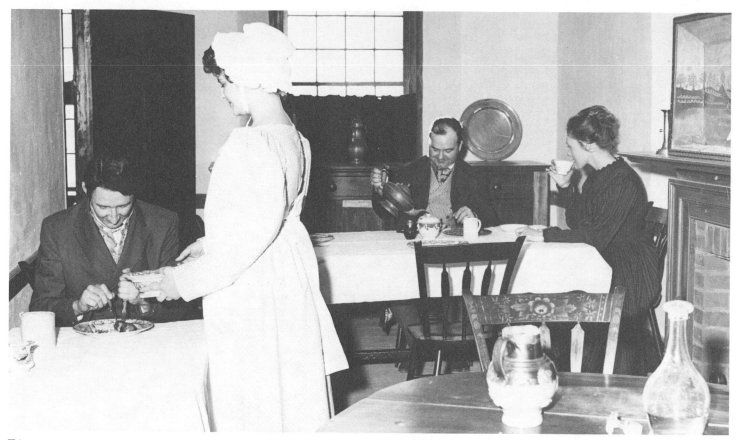

The general store was a perfect place for a restaurant. Since everyone gathered at the store for business and social reasons, it was logical to open a restaurant there. Most of the storekeepers offered home-baked goods in the store, if not whole meals.

Fresh bread and cheese for all the customers at this store!

Yeah! I love to play checkers! The next move is mine!

As the storekeeper sorts mail, he listens in to the hot political debate carried on by two of his customers. An election is coming up and the storekeeper has all the latest newspapers to keep the villagers up-to-date on the latest campaign promises. Can you see a spittoon?

Everyone in the village came to the store to meet. Sometimes some of the young villagers took advantage of the storekeeper's friendliness. In this picture Mrs. McCormick scolds a young man for his bad behavior, while one of his rude friends steals an apple.

Solving community problems

Town meetings were held at the village store. Farmers met there to talk about problems with their crops. Ladies planned community social events. If there wasn't a church or school in the village yet, the general store was a temporary place of prayer and learning.

Watch your aim!

Children loved to play on the porch of the store. Men sat around the stove and smoked their pipes or chewed tobacco.

Chewing tobacco became more and more popular. The men bit a small piece of tobacco off a "plug", which was a big piece. As they chewed the tobacco, a dark liquid, which looked like licorice, formed in their mouths. They would spit this tobacco into a bucket called a "spittoon" or "cuspidor". If they missed, the storekeeper's children had to clean the floor. There was a story of one storekeeper's wife who chased a man out of her store with a broom because his aim was so poor!

The two men in this picture are asking the storekeeper's advice on a contract they are about to make between them. The storekeeper was often involved in business deals as a witness and an advisor. He knew more about laws than most of the other villagers.

The mail coach has just left. The villagers are lining up to get their mail from the store-keeper. The store is busy today. Mrs. Gibson is choosing material for a new dress while her husband chats with some friends by the stove. A toddler keeps her eyes on the dog!

The storekeeper was many people in one

The storekeeper or merchant was always one of the most important people in town. He or she had many jobs to do and had to do them well.

The politician

The merchant was usually elected to the town council. He knew everyone and everyone knew him. He knew about what was happening in the community because people were constantly discussing their business in his store. He often traveled to the city to trade his goods. He had more contact with the outside world than anyone else in the community.

The businessman

Most business deals were made at the general store. Most of the farmers and villagers needed contact with the merchant in their business. Craftsmen sold their products at the store. The miller sold his flour there. The farmers traded their goods there.

The accountant

The storekeeper had to have a good mind for arithmetic. He kept track of what everyone owed in the community. He had to be careful that people did not cheat him. The storekeeper was also the banker. He had to know what goods and services were worth so that no one would be cheated. He had to be able to decide what he needed to order to restock his shelves. He had to know how much postage to charge on incoming letters.

The storekeeper looks at some new books in the city. His customers wait for him to bring back the latest novels. He has chosen a book by Charles Dickens. Dickens was a favorite author in Europe and North America. His stories were published in magazines as well.

The lawyer

The storekeeper had to know about laws. Often he was the person who helped to make contracts between people. He was the village lawyer.

The news-bringer

On his trips to the city the merchant heard news from all over the world. He learned about new products, new fashions and new ways of doing things. He brought the news back to the village. In those days the newspapers were not delivered from door to door. There was usually only one copy of the paper for the whole community to share. The paper was found in the store. Everyone came in to read the paper and discuss the news outside the village.

The diplomat

The merchant had to be careful not to offend his customers. He had to be friendly even if he had reason not to be. One day a man came into a store to buy a bag of wool. His wife was going to spin the wool into yarn to knit socks for the winter. The storekeeper weighed the wool. He turned his back for a moment to figure out how much the man owed. While his back was turned, the man grabbed a big piece of cheese and hid it in the wool. The storekeeper saw what the man did out of the corner of his eye.

He faced a problem. He couldn't accuse the man of stealing! He asked the man if he

could weigh the wool again because he thought he had made a mistake. Sure enough, the bag weighed three times as much as before. The man ended up paying much more than if he had just bought the cheese. The storekeeper did not embarrass his customer. Hopefully, he taught him a lesson!

Everyone's friend

It was important for the storekeeper to be friendly. People would want to go to the store more often. Because the settlers were so self-sufficient, they did not have to make many trips to the store. They could make almost everything they needed right in their own homes. However, because the general store was such a fun place to go to and the merchant was usually friendly, people wanted to make more trips to the store. Being a friendly storekeeper was important for good business.

*Most stores were owned and operated by families. Both the mother and father had the same duties as storekeepers. However, although both shared the same duties, the people in the community referred to the husband as the "merchant" or "storekeeper". Therefore, we have used the pronoun "he" when we talk about the early storekeeper. If the father died, the mother took over the whole responsibility of running the store unless there was a son or daughter old enough to share it with her.

This corner of the general store contains hardware goods. Andrea buys some turpentine for her father. Judie gives her change. When money was used at the store it was kept in a cash register like the one in the picture. Judie helps out in the store every day after school. Most of her friends also had chores to do around their farms each day.

Debbie loves to work in the store. Her jobs include weighing goods, sweeping, grinding the coffee and serving the customers. She loves being the storekeeper's daughter. All her friends, including many good-looking young men, drop into the store regularly.

Running the store was a family affair

The merchant's whole family worked in the store. There was a lot to keep everyone busy. The wife of the merchant performed many of the same duties as her husband did. She weighed the goods, served the customers and helped them to make decisions about what they wanted to buy. She kept the ladies up to date on the newest fashions.

Chores galore

One of the merchant's children usually became the next storekeeper. However, all the children worked in the store every day. There were many chores to be done. They had to sweep out the store, unload and load the farmers' wagons, polish the brass weigh scales and dust the shelves. The biggest job of the week was helping to prepare for Saturday, the busiest shopping day. Many of the foodstuffs at the store were bought by the storekeeper in bulk. For example, he would buy oatmeal in large sacks or barrels. The merchant sold food in bulk as well, but in smaller amounts. His children weighed the food and divided it into smaller amounts. Often customers would ask which child weighed which bag. Some were known for being more generous than others.

The older sons and daughters learned to keep the accounts for their father and mother. If the father went on a buying trip, the son or daughter carried on the business for the storekeeper.

Tom, the storekeeper's son, is helping to load some bags of grain to be taken to the mill. The grain will be ground into flour there. While Tom is at the mill, he meets some friends who "double-dare" him to do something he will later regret. Read the story on the next page to find out what it was!

Judie dusts the shelves before she goes to school in the morning.

Debbie gives the floor a good sweep. She is expecting the miller's son to deliver some flour today. She has baked some fresh biscuits to offer him when he comes.

A painful new experience

The storekeeper's children had an advantage over the other children in the community. They had a chance to try new products from the cities.

One day Tom, the storekeeper's son, was swimming at the mill pond with his friends from the village. Tom's friends decided they wanted to try some chewing tobacco. They dared Tom to sneak some to them. Tom took the dare and came running back with a plug of tobacco. The boys chewed to their hearts' content, but did not know enough to spit the juice and tobacco out. Moans of pain were heard throughout the village that night. One of the moans came from the bedroom of the merchant's son over the village store!

Even grandfather helps out in the store. He is washing the windows to allow in lots of light. He is proud of the family store!

The farmer has unloaded his wagon. He puts his empty basket back. The goods he bought have been packed inside the wooden chest on the wagon. The storekeeper says goodbye at the door.

The general store from the outside

The general store was usually a two-storey building centrally located in the village. The front of the store usually had two big display windows with a door in the center. One window displayed items of interest for females. In it were hats, material, scissors, buttons and dolls. In the other window, articles such as tools and shoes were displayed for men.

Often there were awnings over the windows to prevent the sun's rays from coming into the store. The sun would have faded the materials and melted the butter. The awnings also provided shade for the villagers who sat on the benches in front of the store.

Most general stores had platforms or wooden sidewalks built in front of them. In those days roads were not paved. The platform cut down on the dirt that was tracked into the store. When farmers pulled their wagons up to the store it was easier for them to unload onto the platform. Often the platform was the same height as the wagon. The farmer did not have to lift bags, barrels and parcels. He simply transferred them onto the platform, thereby saving his back from injury.

There were usually two posts on either side of the platform called "hitching posts". Horses and wagons were tied to the posts. There was always a sign at the front of the store. It was painted by hand. It was colorful to attract customers.

The storekeeper displays some of his merchandise in front of the store. The right side of the store has been made into a barber shop. The merchant's son is the barber.

This old general store was opened in 1723. Villagers sit on the platform discussing the latest village news.

General stores were always cluttered. Everything a person could need was sold there. People sat around in the store chatting, reading, or just keeping warm by the stove.

Let the storekeeper show you around

One of the best words to describe the inside of the general store is "cluttered". Everything the storekeeper had to offer was put on display.

The cosiest spot

In the center of the store there was a big wood-burning pot-belly stove. There was no central heating then. The stove heated the store in winter. It also provided a cosy spot for card games, checkers and great conversations.

Barrels, boxes and bags

At the rear of the store there were tubs of pickles, tobacco and crackers and closed barrels of vinegar and molasses. There were containers of wood in which items were shipped to the store. Cardboard boxes were not yet used. In addition, during transport from the city to the general store, the wooden barrels kept things from breaking.

Mail and accounts

In one corner of the store was the post office. Villagers came here to send and to pick up mail. The storekeeper had a small office area at the back of the store. This is where he or she kept records of what people owed.

Bins, tins, jars and scales

Along one side of the store was a long counter. Behind it there were shelves which went from floor to ceiling. There were built-in bins containing coffee, tea, peas, rice, dried fruit and oatmeal. These bins were behind the counter. There were also smaller drawers of pepper, cinnamon, cloves and other spices. On the counter stood large brass scales. Everything that was sold in the store was weighed on these. Tin-covered glass containers lined the counter. All sorts of treats, such as licorice sticks, stick candy and wax gums could be found in these. The shelves behind the counter were filled with china, glassware and silverware.

The storekeeper records a barter in the accounts book. There was usually a small office area somewhere in the store.

The candy counter was the most popular spot in the store for children and their grandmothers.

These built-in bins contain coffee, tea and the many spices which gave the store its wonderful aroma.

These small scales weigh by balance. The storekeeper balances the produce on the right with the weight on the left.

Judie and her mother examine some lace carefully before they sell it to the customer. It is very important not to find any flaws, as it will soon become a neighbor's wedding dress.

Pins, buttons, shoes and combs

Along the other side of the store ran a long bare counter. On this counter women could unroll bolts of material to look for flaws. This counter was known as the "dry goods" counter. One could find combs, pins, buttons, shoes, tools, eye-glasses and mirrors here. No space was wasted in a general store. Even the ceiling was used. From it hung lamps, tools and even children's carriages.

Music to the nose

The store was filled with a wonderful blend of aromas. If one stood in the store long enough, one could smell molasses, coffee, cheese, fruit, vinegar and spices. Together the aroma was like an orchestra making beautiful music to the nose!

This corner of the store was used twice a week by the visiting dressmaker.

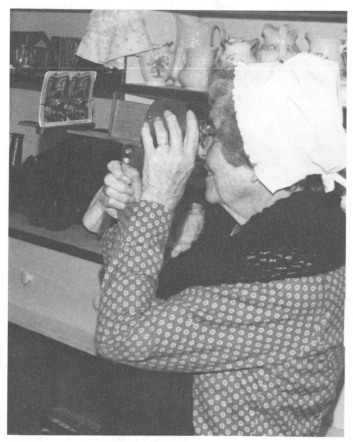

This stereoscopic viewer shows the two pictures you see as one 3-D image.

"I love to turn the wheel and I especially love the smell of fresh-ground coffee!"

The storekeeper shows how men with mustaches can keep them dry while drinking.

All space was used in the store. Items that hung high could be reached with this stick.

This gadget is a donut cutter. As it rolls over the dough the middle part makes the hole. The oval shapes the donut. The storekeeper picked up this invention on his last trip to the city. His customers will love this one!

Did you know that sugar came from the West Indies in cones? A piece was then cut off and sold to a customer.

Clay jars were used to take liquids such as honey, vinegar and molasses home.

Nothing was wasted by the pioneers. Eel fat was drained into the grooves of this fryer and used for making candles.

Remember! When your supplies run low, my general store is the place to go!

The storekeeper is showing a turkey to the customer. It is near Thanksgiving, so turkeys and geese are in great demand. Are the products in this picture groceries or produce?

General stores contained dry goods, groceries and produce all in one room.

The store traded goods

There were two kinds of goods found at the general store; goods to be traded with and goods to be traded for. The items traded *with* were mainly farm products. The items traded *for* were mainly goods that could not be found in the community. Below are two lists of goods. Which list is the list of goods traded *with*? Which is the list of products traded *for*?

List One	List Two
sugar	flour
spices	pork
fruit	butter
molasses	honey
rum	beef
iron goods	eggs
drugs	chickens
china	ducks
powder	geese
silk	hides
satin	fruit
dye	syrup
rice	wool
tea	goose feathers
buttons	soap
coffee	cider

There is one item which appears on both lists. Can you think why?

Most of the goods in the two lists opposite were available at the store. If someone wanted something special, such as a new bonnet or toy, the storekeeper could order it. These ordered goods could take from one to three months to arrive.

Dry goods, groceries and produce

The goods, such as hardware goods and dishes and combs were called "dry goods". Teas, coffees, peppercorns, mace, nutmeg and other spices that came from faraway places were called "groceries". Fresh fruit, eggs, vegetables and other foods from the nearby farms were called "produce".
Cans started to show up on general store shelves about one hundred years ago. One could buy a few items, such as shrimps, oysters and sardines in cans, but these were usually very special items. Tobacco came in tins and there were a few other groceries, such as baking powder, tea and some coffees in tins. However, tins and cans were found in the later stores, not in the early pioneer community stores.

Most stores did not have to advertise because competition was small. This advertisement appeared in the paper of a larger town. There were two or three grocery stores in this town and each tried to get all the business it could. The names of the products this store sold were written on the doors of the store. The products had no brand names. They were listed as eggs, bacon and so on. The products came in large barrels and sacks. Everyone comes shopping carrying their own baskets in which they will take their shopping home.

The goods in these barrels and bins would today be packaged in bright cans and boxes.

Buying then and buying now

Stores did not advertise their products the way they do today. Most stores just had a list of what was available. One creative storekeeper made up a poem listing the products he sold.

Salt pork and powder shot and flint
Cheese, sugar, rum and peppermint
Tobacco, raisin, flour and spice,
Flax, cotton, wool and sometimes rice!

Oatmeal was oatmeal

Today many companies make the same product. Cereals are found in all different forms. They have many different names, shapes and types of packages. In the early days there was no variety. Oatmeal was oatmeal and the only way it could be bought was in big barrels.

Did price mean quality?

If a customer wanted to buy socks, there was usually only one type available in the store. One storekeeper tried an experiment. He put three pairs of the same socks on display with different price tags. A customer came in, felt each pair and bought the pair with the most expensive price tag. He said he could always tell good quality!

Why do we buy today?

Do you think people today buy according to price? Conduct a poll! Interview some friends and neighbors. Ask them why they buy the brands they do. Why do they buy certain foods, makes of clothes, hardware, toys? Make a chart! List all your articles in the left-hand column. Across the top, put the reasons for buying. These can be some of the following; high price, low price, brand name, place of purchase, appearance or packaging or advertising.

For example, if a neighbor says she bought a cereal because it looked good and was on sale, you would tick off "low price" and "packaging". If your parents buy products at the supermarket because they like the quality and the price, you would mark "low price" and "quality". Add up your check-marks. What conclusions have you reached about people's shopping habits today?

"Warner's Safe Nervine is the one I pick for sores or pains or if my dog has ticks! It heals, it cures, it relieves the pain. It is there to use again and again."

Many tonics and pills could be bought in the 1800s even though little was known about medicine. Can you see a bedpan, hot-water bottle and a pill maker?

Cure-all tonics

The only products which had brand names in the early days were tonics and medicines. Tonics promised to cure almost every ailment from corns to stomach pains. In truth, most of the tonics were made of the same ingredients. Quinine and alcohol were the main ingredients. Each family favored one tonic over another. The tonics had names such as "Dr. Jones' Fabulous Cure-all" and "Dr. Haley's Elixir and Tonic".

Curing man or beast

One storekeeper favored "Warner's Safe Nervine". His daughter was dusting shelves one day when she slipped and cut herself on some broken glass. Her father reached for the Warner's and put some on the cut. Later that day his son brought in his sick dog. The storekeeper gave the dog a spoonful. The day before, the storekeeper had taken a spoonful himself to soothe an upset stomach. The same tonic that was used for people was also used for animals. The medicine that was taken by mouth was also used as an ointment for cuts and sores.

Two popular illnesses

Medicine had not improved much from one hundred years before. (See the earlier pages on the Apothecary.) Bleeding and amputations were still used as remedies. No one knew much about the causes of illnesses. However, many medicines were now packaged in bottles. The names of the diseases were different from diseases today. "Catarrh" and "ague" were two sicknesses which often kept the settlers down. Catarrh was a phlegm in the back of the throat. Ague was like a flu, with fever and chills. Ague was thought to be caused by working in the fields. People felt it had something to do with the turning over of the soil. People who worked in the woods or away from cultivated areas supposedly did not come down with ague. When a settler wanted to cure an illness, he or she either mixed up a tonic or bought a favorite bottled tonic at the general store. There was usually quite a large apothecary section in each store because so many tonics were available for sale.

Most people used the barter system at the general store. It was not surprising that when people wanted to pay cash, the storekeeper examined the bills carefully. He did not get very much money in the store, so he made sure that the bills he got were not counterfeit.

How the barter system worked

Most of the settlers in a pioneer community used the barter system instead of money. Instead of taking money to do the shopping as we do today, the settlers would gather up things they grew on their farms and trade them for items in the store. Trade products were sometimes known as "country pay". Little money was used because farmers did not earn wages. They just grew their crops and traded them for things they needed.

Bartering meant trading one product for another of equal value. However, it was difficult for farmers to trade for equal value amongst each other. Someone always owed something to somebody. There had to be a record kept of who owed what to whom. The general store made the barter system work. Instead of trading with each other, everyone brought their goods to the general store. The storekeeper added up what was brought in and what was taken from the store. He kept a record of what people owed or how much credit they had.

Credits and debits

Today when we open an account at the bank, the money we put in is called a "credit". The money we take out is called a "debit". The general store was like a bank. Instead of payments of money, people received their money's worth in goods from the store. The goods that were brought into the store were "credited" to the farmer or settler who brought the goods in. This meant that the merchant owed the settler that amount in goods from his store. When the settler took goods, those goods were "debited" from his account. He owed that amount to the storekeeper. The following are examples of some typical barters in the store.

Barter one

A farmer buys lumber from the sawmill. He pays the sawyer in flour, pork and butter. The sawyer pays his men with the goods that the farmer brought in. The goods the workers do not need are taken to the general store and traded for other goods, such as coffee, sugar and cloth.

Barter two

Customer Edith Liddell gave the storekeeper:

5 chickens	a large ham
1 duck	a basket of apples
3 geese	50 eggs

In return, the storekeeper gave:

buttons	ammonia
tea	cream of tartar
sugar	lamp glass
currants	coal oil
cornstarch	peppermint
tobacco	a clock

The goods Edith received were equal in value to what she gave except for two chickens. She now had two chickens to her credit. The storekeeper wrote the credit in his book. She will receive goods for it on her next visit to the store.

The merchant was the banker

When money was used, the general store merchant acted as the banker in the village. He loaned money to farmers and they in turn paid him back when the crops were in. The farmer paid interest either in money, or in additional crops. When the farmer had extra money, the storekeeper or merchant stored the money in a big iron safe. He paid the farmer a small interest. He then used the money to make loans to others in the community. He charged more interest on the money he loaned out.

The storekeeper let settlers run up bills. He kept track of what everyone owed. The bill was usually settled once a year after the harvest was finished. If the crops the farmer brought in were not enough to pay for the bill, the farmer could pay the merchant by doing jobs for him in the store. He could also work for the miller or the sawyer, who then would settle the farmer's account with the storekeeper.

Pioneers needed each other

Today everything is done with money. People do not have to depend on each other as much. Banks lend money, supermarkets provide food and everything can be bought and sold. The barter system kept the pioneer community together. People had to rely on each other much more in the early days. The general store provided a meeting place for people to work out their deals and problems.

Even though food was hard to keep, the early settlers ate well. There were a lot of animals on each farm, so there was not a shortage of fresh meat. This family is enjoying turkey, vegetables and fresh fruit for Sunday dinner. It was a custom to put all the food on the table at once instead of serving it in courses, such as salad, soup, main dish and dessert.

Each year many deaths were caused by food poisoning, especially in the cities. The Departments of Health passed regulations on food quality. Here an inspector holds a spot inspection. The inspector is asking the police behind him to charge the merchant with selling spoiled goods. The merchant tries to give excuses to escape the stiff fine.

Quality, preservation and packaging

In the early days the quality of goods was not tested by the government. Today products are regularly tested and must pass strict standards. In the early days people often bought bad products. There was no refrigeration. Butter could be sold rancid and runny. One woman complained she had to pick bugs out of the oatmeal before her family could eat it. A storekeeper was angry that the crackers he bought were always broken, dirty and damp.

Stopping food from spoiling

Keeping food from going bad was a serious problem for the early settler and for the storekeeper. Since there was no electricity there could be no refrigeration without ice. In the summer no ice could be found. In the heat, food, especially meat, goes bad, smells terrible and can not be eaten. Some ways were found to prevent meat from going bad. Today preservatives are added to foods to make them last longer. In the days of the settlers, meat was packed in salt, smoked in the smokehouse,

pounded and dried in the sun, or pickled in vinegar. The taste of the meat changed, but the meat lasted longer.

The storekeeper stored food such as butter, eggs and vegetables in a root cellar which was always cool. It was underground and the sun could not heat it up. However, it did not do the job that refrigeration does today, so the problem of spoilage was an everyday problem.

Bring your own baskets

There was no special packaging to prevent eggs from breaking against each other. Today eggs are separated from each other in cartons made of cardboard and styrofoam. Back then, eggs were packed in buckets of oatmeal to prevent them from cracking.

The storekeeper did not provide plastic bags for the customers in which to take home their groceries. Customers used their own clay pots, baskets and wooden crates to carry their bought goods home.

Mrs. Williams' daughters are learning the secrets of making good butter. The churn must be clean as a whistle, the cream must be fresh, and all the buttermilk has to be washed out of it. It takes a lot longer to make really good butter, but people stand in line for it at the store! Mrs. Williams should teach Mrs. Black her secret!

Customer relations

The one thing that really bothered some storekeepers about the barter system was that they had to trade the same amount for the same products with each customer. For example, one lady would come in with creamy, salted butter while another would bring in runny, dirty butter. The storekeeper felt he had to allow the same amount for both ladies. It would have been bad manners to insult the lady with the runny butter by giving her less for it.

The dirty butter barter

One day Mrs. Black came to the store with a tubful of butter to trade. She was well-known for the poor butter she made. The storekeeper was upset because he knew he had to trade with her to avoid hard feelings, although he would probably have to throw the butter out.

Two days later, Mrs. Black came back into the store all in a dither. She explained that people dropped in for a visit and that she would need some extra butter. "Well", the storekeeper said, "aren't you lucky! I haven't sold the butter you brought in the other day!" Mrs. Black was not pleased, but what could she say? Her dirty butter barter backfired!

The better butter barter

Not all storekeepers, however, worried about the feelings of every customer. One storekeeper rewarded the special efforts of some of his customers, even if it offended people like Mrs. Black. There was one lady in the community who brought the storekeeper the best butter he'd ever eaten. Mrs. Williams took extra care to churn her butter twice a week while the cream was still fresh. She scrubbed the butter churn thoroughly before each use and washed every bit of buttermilk out of the butter. She made the best butter in the whole area. People tried to buy it as soon as it came into the store. The storekeeper allowed her double the usual butter value on her barter. He in turn sold the butter for double his usual price.

Cheating on both sides

Because quality controls were few in those days, people tried to cheat the storekeeper and sometimes the storekeeper tried to cheat the customers. Some customers found plaster in their flour, ordinary beans that were dyed black in their coffee and sawdust in their oatmeal. Farmers also did their share of cheating. Often the quality of the produce they brought in was poor. Sometimes their grain was not ripe. As new regulations were passed by the Departments of Health, new gadgets were invented to allow people to test for the quality of a product. Mr. Langston, the storekeeper below, shows a grain-grader.

The gadget above was used to grade the quality of grain. The storekeeper had a chart which gave the standard weights of good grain of a certain volume.

The young bride from the city asks the storekeeper for enough ingredients to bake one cake. She does not yet realize that she has to buy her food in large quantities here.

Trips to the village store

Quite often people lived on farms miles away from the village. There were no cars or trains back then to take them into town so they had to rely on an ox-cart and horse-drawn wagons in the summer and horse-drawn sleighs in winter. Because of the long distances and because the roads were so poor, the trip to the village could take up to four hours or more. Most people could probably make the trip once a week.

However, some people did not come to town more than once every couple of months.

It was especially difficult for women to get to the store because they had to look after the children while their husbands did the shopping. Every once in a while however, the whole family would come. It was a special time that the whole family looked forward to!

A sticky situation

One day a woman came to the store with three children, all under the age of six. They hadn't been at the store in four months. The mother was as excited as her children were! As the poor storekeeper tried to wait on the mother, who could not make up her mind about anything, her children ran wild in the store. They looked into all the barrels and pulled things off the shelves. The mother was so thrilled about all the lovely goods in the store that she did not even glance at her children. Without the storekeeper noticing it, the children went to the back of the store and opened the spout on the barrel of molasses. After they left, the storekeeper needed to get something from the back of the store. It was then that he noticed he was standing ankle-deep in sticky molasses! He hoped he would not see that family in his store for at least another four months!

The city bride learns a lesson

Usually when a farmer came to town to trade he would trade for enough goods to last his family for a while so he would not have to come to town for a few weeks. One day a young woman came to town to do her shopping. She had never lived on a farm before. She gave her shopping list to the storekeeper for him to fill the order. She wanted a quarter cup of butter, a half teaspoon of vanilla, a cup of sugar, one egg, two cups of flour and a cup of milk. The storekeeper chuckled when he saw her list. The young bride had ordered enough ingredients to bake a cake. She had to learn that in the country people bought goods in "bulk". Their shopping had to last them for at least a couple of weeks!

A new world for children

The general store was particularly interesting for children. Most children had been born on the farms where they lived. The farthest distance they ever traveled was from the farm to the village. They did not have any experience of the rest of the world. The general store held a magic key that could open up the rest of the world to them. They could imagine sailing to Ceylon and India for teas and silks. They could dream of flying dragon kites with children in China. They could experience another part of the world by smelling the spices that came from there.

It was not unusual to find little noses in the bins of imported spices!

Every child looked forward to the trip to the general store. There was always a treat waiting there. There was a world of licorice sticks and Turkish delight to delight every child. The only unpleasant task was dividing up the candy when the children got home. Someone always ended up with a bigger piece than someone else. The parents were left with the arguments!

"Open your mouth and close your eyes! I've been to the store and I have a surprise."

"Load the wagon! Let's get going!"

"Do I smell fresh bread in the oven?"

Kids at large!

"What a heavenly smell! H-m-m-m!"

"I'd love this doll for my birthday!"

"Do you think this bonnet suits me?"

"Jellybeans! Oh, how I love you!"

"I think this is a better move!"

"Oh fiddleheads! I lost again!"

"The smell of cloves reminds me of hot cider, baked ham and pomander balls."

"Bonnets on! It's time to go home. We're sad to leave, but we'll be back soon!"

City markets

The storekeeper received farm produce from the farmers in the community. However, how did the storekeepers come across such articles as tea and refined sugar? When the farmers had traded enough produce from their farm such as flour, butter and eggs, the storekeeper would load his wagon with these things and go to the nearest city. There he would trade cheese, eggs and flour with the merchants in the city who had the goods he wanted. These products were brought to this country from faraway places in ships. Teas came from China and India, coffee from Ceylon and South America and sugar from the West Indies.

Big cities had huge marketplaces where goods could be bought or traded. Many city people bought directly from the country merchants at the market. Then with the money the merchant received, he could buy from other city merchants who had the goods he needed.

The picture above shows the confusion in a city market. There were run-down stalls, broken-down sheds and cluttered wagons. It was hard to keep order and even harder

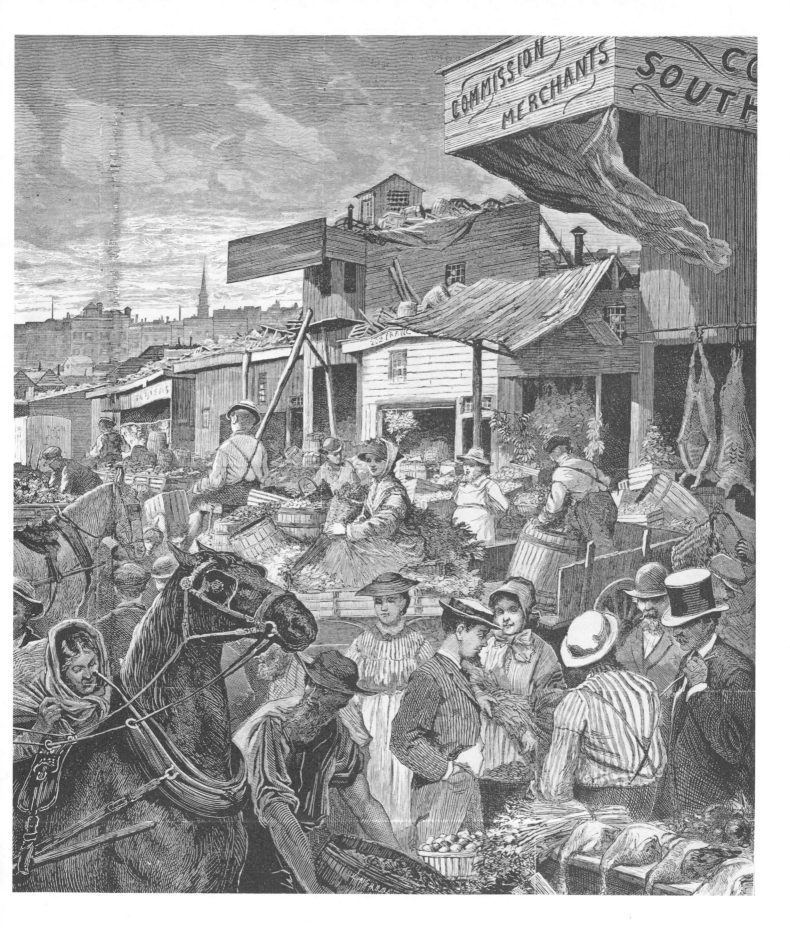

to keep the marketplace clean. The store-keepers from the towns and villages sold their goods here along with many farmers. Many storekeepers sold their produce to the "Commission Merchants", who then sold those same goods to the public at a much higher price. Because there was no refrigeration, many foods were spoiled.

People from the cities went to the country fairs to get fresh meat and vegetables. They also got better prices there. However, these ladies found the meat at this fair a bit too fresh!

The farmer above is loading his wagon with fresh produce. He will not take it to the village store. He prefers to take his meat, vegetables and eggs to the city market to sell them at a higher price there. It takes him about a week to complete his travels and trades.

The best deals in the city and the country

Some farmers, who had good wagons that would carry them to the city safely, took their produce to the city market instead of to the country store. Many farmers felt that they could get better prices themselves at the open city market. One could find hundreds of farmers and merchants coming to the city for market days.

City people also went to country fairs to buy fresh produce. In those days it was important to get the best deal on everything one had to buy.

Farmers, storekeepers and commission merchants alike await the arrival of the ships from faraway places. Ships from the Caribbean and South America have just landed. They have transported sugar, tropical fruit, such as bananas, and rich, dark coffee beans. Merchants sell the goods at the harborfront. These fruits, spices and coffees will travel back to the villages with the farmers and storekeepers. ➤

This cartoon of a traveling merchant showed how he took over the whole town when he came. Everyone was interested in new goods. Many storekeepers never had to go to the city because so many merchants and peddlers traveled the country selling their goods to them.

These traveling peddlers have picked up a pig from one of the farmers. Hopefully, they will sell it in the next town. Some farmers preferred to trade with peddlers instead of the store-keeper, because they felt the goods were newer and fresher. The pig was traded for a clock.

58

In the bigger towns and cities vendors sold meat, fish, vegetables and bread right from their wagons. The woman on the left is testing to see if the fish is fresh. Often it wasn't!

Traveling merchants and peddlers

Many storekeepers did not go to the city to trade their goods. There were traveling merchants who went from village to village and from town to town to sell their goods. These peddlers charged higher prices, but they were welcomed by many storekeepers who did not enjoy going to the city to buy and sell their goods. These peddlers also sold to the villagers directly, sometimes taking away some of the general store's business.

Milk wagons went from house to house in cities and large towns. People had to run out with their pitchers to get milk from the large containers. Milk vendors also sold eggs and vegetables to their customers. Today there are few milkmen left. ➤

More people in the towns meant opening more stores. Even this small town has a butcher, baker, hardware store and millinery. A few years before there was only a general store.

Stores become more specialized

General stores continued to thrive in small country communities. However, as villages grew into towns, the role of the general store became less important. With the building of railroads, people could buy their own goods in the cities. Specialized stores, such as the milliner's shop, the hardware store and the harness shop, opened in the towns. One store could no longer carry all the goods offered from the factories in the cities and large towns.

With the coming of door-to-door mail delivery, people no longer had to go to the general store for their mail. Newspapers advertised all the new products available. New department stores sent out catalogs from which people could order just about anything they needed. As a result, the general store became a place to buy only articles a person needed immediately, such as some foods and tools. Storekeepers even put ads in the local papers to try to keep their customers, but they could not turn back the clock of progress!

How could a general store compete with a hardware store that sold so many items? At the end of the 1800s people had many choices in the goods they bought, such as stoves.

Instead of having their clothes made by the visiting dressmaker at the general store, ladies could now buy dresses and hats right in the millinery shop. One could still have a dress made to order, but it was often more convenient to buy ready-made dresses and hats.

The harness shop of a hundred years ago was like a service station today. Horses were used for transportation then, so people needed saddles, harnesses, straps and whips. Many of the items in the store came from the city, but quite a number were made right in the back shop.

Mott Haven Flour Mills advertises that their Payn's Sure-Raising Flour rises so high that it breaks right through the stove. Other flours can't compete, so they give up and run away.

Competition creates advertising

New machines made it possible to mass-produce almost any item. With the growth of factories near the towns, more stores were needed to sell all the extra goods made. Competition started to grow. Companies had to convince their customers that their products were better than other products on the market. Newspapers began to carry pages and pages of advertisements, all telling about the wonderful benefits of hundreds of different products.

Department stores are born

Stores became bigger and bigger. A person could again go into one store and buy just about anything that he or she could possibly need. The department store was like a huge general store with more choices of each product. Each type of product, such as men's boots or ladies' hats, now had its own special area in the new department store. Shopping became easier and easier for people. Fewer things needed to be made in the home.

In our hearts to stay

Many people had fond memories of afternoons spent at the general store. The cosy atmosphere created by the pot-belly stove, the ringing of the spitoon and the delicious aroma of the many foods and spices can not be found in the big stores. The general store is coming alive again! People all over the country are opening up small country stores so that we too can spend time recalling the days of the early settlers, a time when you knew all your neighbors and met them for a chat at the old store.

More people meant more stores. More stores meant more goods. More of everything meant people had a choice. Competition made it necessary to sell goods cheaper. "Sales" were born!

Large department stores offered many items in one place. Decorated windows invited the shoppers in. Window-shopping was popular.

Advertisements in the papers helped the sales of the many brand name products.

Glossary

ague a flu-like illness
Amish a Mennonite sect
apothecary a druggist
barter system the exchange of goods without the use of money
bin a storage container
brand name the name of a product
bulk a large size, mass or volume
catarrh a swelling of the mucous membranes of the nose and throat
churn a container in which cream is beaten to make butter
Columbus, Christopher an Italian explorer who found America, while searching for India
community a group of people sharing the same services in an area
cooper a craftsperson who makes wooden barrels and tubs
cuspidor a spittoon
eighteenth century 1701 to 1800
foodstuff anything that is food
goods items for sale in a store
groceries foodstuffs other than fresh farm products
harness the leather frame and straps put on horses, oxen for pulling objects
ingredients parts that make up a whole – eggs, flour and milk are cake ingredients
Jamestown one of the first settlements in North America– located in Virginia
Jesuit belonging to the Society of Jesus, a Roman Catholic order
lumber boards cut from trees
Mennonite a member of a Protestant Evangelical sect

merchant a storekeeper
miller the person who owns and runs the grist mill
millinery a hat shop
molasses a dark, thick syrup
peddler a traveling salesperson
pioneer a person who settles in an unsettled area
pomander ball an apple or orange stuck full of cloves and rolled in spices – used for creating a lovely aroma in a closet or a room
poultice a thick paste applied to a swollen or infected area to take down the swelling or absorb the infection
produce fresh farm products, such as fruit and vegetables
Puritan a member of an old Protestant group
quinine a bitter liquid – a basic ingredient of many tonics
seal a stamp used with hot wax to close letters and packages
seventeenth century 1601 to 1700
spittoon a bowl into which people used to spit chewing tobacco
tonic a liquid that was used as a remedy for many illnesses
trading post a store in the wilderness that traded local products for supplies
tump line a strap placed on the forehead to secure a load on a person's back
vendor a person who sells goods
wilderness an unsettled area

Index

Acknowledgements

Library of Congress, Scugog Shores Museum, Port Perry, Century Village, Lang, Colonial Williamsburg, Ministry of Industry and Tourism, Ontario Archives, Metropolitan Toronto Library, New York Historical Association, Upper Canada Village, Harper's Weekly, Marc Crabtree, Peter Crabtree, Bobbie Kalman, Black Creek Pioneer Village.

6789 BP Printed in Canada 09